Culinary Roots 2

a legacy of faith, family and food

Published by Pecan Tree Publishing, November, 2018

Hollywood, Florida

www.pecantreebooks.com

This book or parts thereof may not be reproduced in any form, stored in a retrieval system or transmitted in any form by any means – electronic, mechanical, photocopy, recording or otherwise – without prior written permission of the published, author or legal representative of both parties, except as provided by United States of America copyright law.

Copyright © 2018 Brenda L. Jackson

ISBN: 978 1 7328311 2 4

Library of Congress Control Number: 2018959198

All rights reserved.

Culinary Roots 2
a legacy of faith, family and food

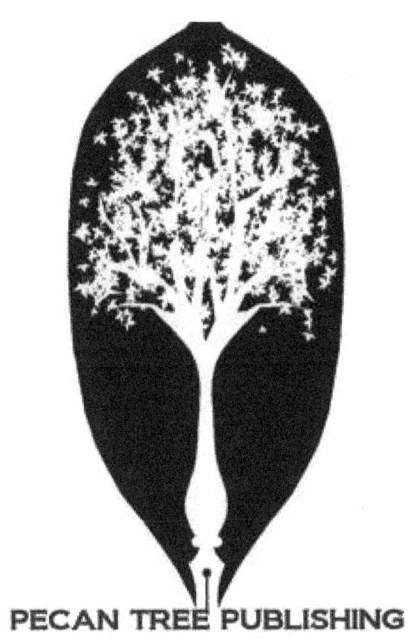

PECAN TREE PUBLISHING

Brenda L. Jackson

Pecan Tree Publishing

Hollywood, Florida

786.763.1295

www.pecantreebooks.com

Email: info@pecantreebooks.com

Photography:
Angelica Velez, Ixty, LLC
Ashley Jackson, Black Royal Family Productions

Book Cover and Layout:
Angelica Velez, Ixty, LLC

Artwork:
Jeremy Jackson

Culinary Roots Kitchen Lab:
Jonathan Jackson

Dedication

In memory and honor of my baby sister, Beverly Ann Jackson (Bev).

December 21, 2014, was the life journey end for my sister. In the prior two years, Beverly and her children's ordinary days became the opposite. Beverly birthed, protected, instructed, chastised, encouraged and taught (by example), her three babies. – Jeremy, Jonathan, and Ashley. Those babies are now adults; and they continue to flourish from all that their mother placed in their hearing and their spirit. They each contributed creatively to this cookbook with photography, film production, art/illustration as well as taste testing in the Culinary Roots Kitchen Lab.

My sister was a character. As with any baby sister, she was aggravating at times, but funny, most of the time. She took leaps of faith in all that she accomplished. Each day she took opportunities to make a better life for herself and her children.

Beverly loved teaching, although that was not her profession. She was the youth Sunday school teacher when we attended Solomon's Temple. When we were kids, her playtime would be running a school with imaginary students. She even took attendance (yes, of imaginary students). You may ask, who answered when she called the names of her students, of course, she would respond. She would remain silent to ensure an accurate count of those students that were absent. I can't make this stuff up!

Bev was a dreamer and a prayer warrior. She had a God-given gift and she used this gift to encourage, teach and enlighten all who crossed her path. She was a teacher beyond her imaginary school and students. I believe it was her time of preparation during her childhood that allowed her to be ready for her children, her family, her co-workers and others.

Bev added value to someone's life every day. Her last two years were not easy and not without pain. She never told me the full extent of her pain nor what was happening inside her body. The days when we spoke, I now know she was preparing me and the rest of the family for her leaving us. She knew peace and relief was soon to come to her body and mind.

I'm grateful and oh so blessed for the time we had together. Even now, I continue to learn from her, which says a lot with her being the baby girl. I miss her so, but remember the times and still smile thinking of our rushing home to change into our play clothes – yes in my day, we had certain clothes we wore for playtime. For the sake of clarity, take off my school clothes – put on my play clothes – go outside to play kickball, hop scotch, jump rope and box ball (a/k/a 4-square).

Life is a journey and death is part of that journey. I choose to remember and celebrate the life of my baby sis - whom I love. Bev is at peace as she journeyed to the ultimate perfection – heaven.

Beverly Jackson

Jeremy Orlando Jackson

Jonathan Reid Jackson

Ashley Victoria Jackson

Foreword

In most African American homes, the kitchen is the cornerstone. The same can be said for Caribbean, Latin/Hispanic, Italian, Southern and other cultures where food and family are one. The kitchen is where the expression of love and family tradition takes place. For my family, Mama would be in the kitchen with her apron on and I would be cracking the eggs, snapping peas or shucking corn, depending on which dishes were planned. The aroma would have everyone anticipating the moment we would say grace and grub. The greater joy was - and is topping the wonderful culinary experience with good wholesome conversation and laughter; ending with all giving compliments to the cook. It's an experience that was once passed down through generations; sadly, it is now often taken for granted or is a mere memory.

When I sit down for a meal at the table of Brenda Jackson, I feel like I'm experiencing years of tradition coming from her mother and father and their family roots. It's an experience that makes me feel like all is not lost in the family value system. I'm reminded that some people still take pleasure in their culinary roots and will continue to pass down those recipes and secrets that made their dishes special. Brenda gives each recipe her own unique twist and then plates them with some of her unique creations. To hear Brenda describe the menu selection is much like that of a waiter at a five-star restaurant giving you the chef's daily specials. My mouth starts to water, and I get a vivid picture of what will be served and without doubt enjoyed. I vividly see the colors and plating just from her verbal description. And watching her cook is amazing. With every chop of the knife and every stir, there's a pleasant smile and a serene expression on her face that makes you believe she is destined for this. She was designed to make sure that some values are not lost; and by sharing these precious gems she can contribute to reminding society of the importance of a family sitting together at the dinner table.

We live in a time when everything is fast moving. Microwave ovens, drive-thru fast food and boxed meals have become the norm. So, it's refreshing to see that Brenda Jackson has embraced the tradition of our ancestors and made dinner time an experience and an expression of love. Whether she's feeding two people or catering for 20, she takes pride in every detail. And at the end of the experience everyone says, "Wow that was delicious!" (If they're able to speak!) And then comes the radiant smile on her face and a simple, "Thank you." But the joy inside I'm sure is quite fulfilling, as is accomplishing her mission of giving those dining with her a memorable experience.

My prayer is that this collection of recipes will bless every home that it enters; and that it would restore the great joys of family time. The cornerstone of the family with sons and daughters helping mom and dad with dinner; families engaging in conversation and togetherness that come along with it. Most rewarding of all is being able to share these recipes with your children and your children's children and preserving the value of preparing a home-cooked meal.

Anita Wilson

The M.O.V.E.M.E.N.T. Worldwide

This Journey That I Embrace

Acknowledgements

Life is a journey; and I am forever grateful for where my path is leading. I will never know what is ahead for me until I reach the next destination. While at my there, I will embrace and learn from the journey. I cannot promise to do everything correctly, because life is teaching me with each arrival and departure.

While speaking the words thank you, will never equate to what my heart declares, thank you, still to the following:

Emily Claudette Freeman, Publisher and Editor of Pecan Tree Publishing, whose presence and willingness to have impromptu lengthy telephone meetings continues to push me to my place of blessings.

Bishop Victor T. Curry, D.Min., D.Div., Founding Senior Pastor/Teacher, New Birth Baptist Church Cathedral of Faith International. Bishop Curry, my pastor, father in the faith and friend, you are faith in God personified. As you push forward, I will also.

Peeling the Onion Journey (PTOJ), my group of phenomenal women who continue to invest their time, talent and treasure in our pursuit to add value wherever possible. As always, I love me some y'all.

I am blessed and humbled by my inner circle - friends that have been around so long they are family.

To the Reid/Reed and Jackson Families, my love for all of you comes without struggle. The decades of conversations, laughter, and even sorrow, unveils why I am, who I am. Our family perpetuates how to love and live God.

To the Patriarchs and Matriarchs of the Family, thank you for my character, work ethic, straightforwardness and so much more that has been imparted. Your prayers and declarations of faith propelled me to this point and I am so grateful to God for each of you.

Father God, I thank You for Your Son, my Lord and Savior, Jesus Christ. My life is rich with the wealth of so much that it cannot be measured or counted. I seek You with heartfelt determination to follow Your will for my life.

Thank You for the blessing of this, my next opportunity to be intentional.

Culinary Roots 2

Cooking Terms

Caramelize	Slowly cook a food until it turns sweet, nutty and brown
Dice	Cut into small cubes
Dredge	Coat moist foods with a dry ingredient (i.e. flour, bread crumbs) before cooking
Dust	Lightly sprinkling a fine layer of a powdered ingredient (powdered sugar, flour, etc.) onto food
Fold	Combine ingredients using a gentle motion of over and under usually with a rubber or silicone spatula
Meld	Blend or mix together, allowing the flavors to merge and complement each other
Minced	Cut up or grind into very small pieces
Pan Searing	Cooking at high temperature the surface of food (meat, poultry or fish) this process seals in the juices and forms a delicious browned crust
Roast	Cooking method using dry heat where the hot air surrounds the food cooking it evenly on all sides; roasting enhances flavor with the browning of the surface of the food
Rough Cut	Chopping of vegetables in non-unformed sizes and shapes (i.e. potatoes)
Sauté	To cook a food quickly with a minimal amount of oil over relatively high heat
Seeded	Removing of seeds from fruits or vegetables having seeds; useful when cooking with hot peppers such as jalapenos or scotch bonnets – seeding reduces the strength of the heat (cap-sa-i-cin)
Simmer	Specific temperature range for stove top cooking (i.e. soups, stews, rice dishes)
Smothered	Cooking (meat, vegetables or seafood) in a covered pan over low heat with a reasonable amount of liquid
Sweating	Usually when cooking vegetables, this process is a gentle heating of the food in a small amount of oil or butter
Tbsp	Abbreviated, measurement for tablespoon
Tsp	Abbreviated, measurement for teaspoon
Whip	Beating an ingredient vigorously to incorporate air which makes the ingredient frothy (i.e. egg whites)

Index

Grace Prayer..........................1

Banana Pudding......................5

Beverly's Sweet Potato Bread Pudding.....7

Blueberry Doobie.....................9

Bubba Ham..........................11

Crockpot Stewed Turtle...............13

Curried Sweet Potato Salad...........15

Daddy's Hamburger and Gravy.........19

Easy Salmon Pasta...................21

Field Peas and Snaps.................23

Fish Curry..........................25

Grace Prayer........................26

Fried Bologna Sandwich..............29

Fried Cabbage......................31

Fried Chicken Gizzards...............37

Frittata.............................39

Green Beans and White Potatoes......41

Hodge Podge Oven Jambalaya.........43

Mac and Cheese CR2.0...............45

Mustard and Turnips.................47

Pancetta And Cheddar Biscuits........49

Peach Cobbler......................53

Grace Prayer.......................54

Perlo Rice..........................57

Pork 'n Beans and Sausage...........59

Potato Crusted Salmon...............63

Roasted Vegetable Feast.............65

Rutabagas..........................67

Skillet Cornbread....................71

Smothered Grits....................73

Stewed Neckbones and Potatoes......75

Summer Salad......................77

Watermelon Cucumber Salad.........79

Grace Prayer

"O taste and see that the LORD is good." Psalm 34:8

Most Gracious and Heavenly Father, we come before You to first give You the honor and the glory and the praise. Father, we praise You because You are holy and sovereign and righteous. For You are GOD, and GOD alone; there is none like You. We praise You for being so good to us.

Father, You said that we can come boldly before Your throne of Grace. So, Father I come now boldly asking for Your grace, Your unmerited favor for this Author Brenda L. Jackson and her book Culinary Roots II. I thank You for giving her the vision, the knowledge and the gift to bless so many. I pray that this book - page by page - word by word blesses families all over the world.

Father, You said in Your word in Third John 1:2, "Beloved, I wish above all things that thou mayest prosper and be in health, even as thy soul prospereth." Father, I pray that this book prospers everyone in their health, in their spirit, and in their soul. I pray that this book leaves a legacy for generations to come and that each recipe blesses Your people and makes them stronger and healthier in their lives and in their faith.

Father, I thank You for Brenda L. Jackson; continue to bless her and her family. I pray that You give her more than enough in her life. Father continue to give her the vision and the passion to bless Your people through her gift of cooking. Thank You Father for this great book. We shall forever give Your name the glory and the honor. It's in the matchless name of our LORD and Savior JESUS the Christ, we pray. Amen.

William Gipson
Douglasville, GA

Banana Pudding

INGREDIENTS

Custard

½ cup sugar or to taste

2 tbsp flour

2 tsp vanilla extract

4 egg yolks

2 cups evaporated milk

Cookies and Bananas

1 box Nilla Wafers

4-5 ripe bananas, sliced

Meringue

4 Egg whites separated earlier

1 cup Sugar

Shredded Coconut

Serve warm or cold.

PREPARATION

In a medium sauce pan, mix flour and sugar. With a low heat slowly add milk. Be sure to stir constantly while cooking for 10-15 minutes – you want a no-lump custard as the milk blends with the dry ingredients.

Separate 4 eggs (set aside whites for meringue). Mix the egg yolks and slowly pour into the pan, again constantly stirring, while cooking for 3-5 minutes, always checking to make sure the custard is blending well.

Preheat oven to 350 degrees. In a medium size baking dish, prepare a single layer of cookies, a layer of bananas and a single layer of custard, then repeat layers. Top/last layer should be custard.

Using a stand or hand mixer on high speed, beat egg whites, gradually adding sugar. Beat until stiff peaks appear. Apply the meringue on top of the custard, lightly sprinkle with shredded coconut.

Bake for 10 to 15 minutes or until the meringue is golden brown.

Beverly's Sweet Potato Bread Pudding

INGREDIENTS

1 – 28 oz. can sweet potatoes or yams (do not drain)

1 tsp vanilla

1 tsp lemon extract

1 stick butter (melted)

1 cup sugar

2 eggs

1 cup self-rising flour

½ cup condensed milk

½ cup evaporated milk

1 tsp cinnamon

1 tsp nutmeg

PREPARATION

Using a 4-quart pot add canned sweet potatoes (including liquid) on medium heat – bring to a boil. In a large bowl add the potatoes and liquid. Using a potato masher or immersion hand mixer, slowly add and mix the remaining ingredients until smooth and creamy.

Preheat oven to 350 degrees. Pour the potato mixture in a greased (with butter or cooking spray) 9x13 pan. Bake for 40-45 minutes until firm. Allow to cool – place in the refrigerator.

Amazing when eaten cold.

Blueberry Doobie

INGREDIENTS

Dumplings (prepare first)

2 cups flour

1 stick butter (cold)

1 cup evaporated milk (cold)

Blueberry

1 bag frozen blueberries or 2 pints fresh blueberries

1 cup sugar or preferred level of sweetness

1 tsp cinnamon

1 tsp ginger

1 tsp nutmeg

1 cup orange juice

1 tbsp orange zest

Serve hot or cold to your liking.

PREPARATION

Dumplings (prepare first)

Blend flour and butter using a fork or pastry cutter, combining thoroughly until you have a crumb like mixture. Add milk and mix with a fork until a sticky dough forms and pulls together.

Using your hands gather and place dumpling mixture on a cutting board, dusted with flour, pin roll – cutting in any shape desired ¼ inch thick.

Add ingredients in a medium sized sauce pan – bring to a boil. Begin dropping in 2 dumplings at a time when blueberry mixture begins to boil. After all the dumplings are in the pot, reduce heat and simmer until mixture slightly thickens.

Bubba Ham

INGREDIENTS

10 lb ham (bone-in)

1 liter cola

1 tbsp ginger (fresh or ground)

½ cup brown sugar

7-8 oz jar Hoisin sauce

PREPARATION

Place ham in large stock pot; add cola, ginger and brown sugar. If needed, add water to ensure the ham is covered in the liquid mixture. Boil for 30 minutes; then set aside to cool.

Remove ham from the pot, placing it in a roasting pan, add one (1) cup of the liquid mixture to the bottom of the roasting pan. Liberally pour the hoisin sauce on the ham, brushing in the sauce to ensure you coat all exposed sides of the ham.

Garnish with pineapples, cherries or apples if you desire.

Bake at 350 degrees for one (1) hour or until the outer portion of the ham has caramelized.

Garnish with pineapples, cherries or apples if you desire.

Crockpot Stewed Turtle

INGREDIENTS

1 lb. turtle meat*

1 cup flour

1 yellow bell pepper

1 red bell pepper

1 green bell pepper

1 onion

Vegetable juice (enough to cover the meat and vegetables)

2 tbsp complete seasoning

2 tsp black pepper

2 tsp onion powder

2 tsp garlic powder

Red pepper flakes (desired level of heat)

Serve piping hot with cornbread.

PREPARATION

Season turtle meat with pink Himalayan salt and pepper; dredge in flour, lightly coating the meat. Pan sear the meat on all sides, using enough olive oil in your skillet to cover the bottom. Remove meat from the skillet and place in crockpot; add the remaining ingredients.

Cook for 6 hours.

*If you're not a fisherman like my father, Orlando Jackson was and now his sons, Orlarry Sherman and Otis Herman Lee and Orlando Benjamin, have inherited my daddy's passion for fishing, turtle meat can be purchased from stores that specialize in wild game. In a pinch, you can always use beef, chicken or pork, but turtle meat brings a different level of taste – in a good way.

Curried Sweet Potato Salad

INGREDIENTS

- 3 small sweet potatoes (diced)
- 1 cup dried cranberries
- 6 oz low fat peach yogurt
- 2 tsp cinnamon
- 1 tsp nutmeg
- ½ cup raw sugar
- 2 tbsp curry powder
- 2 stalks celery (chopped)
- 2 tbsp orange marmalade
- ½ tsp black pepper

PREPARATION

Chop sweet potatoes into small cubes; boil until slightly tender; drain; add remaining ingredients; chill for an hour or overnight to allow flavors to meld.

A great alternative to the standard white potato salad.

Complements great with roasted or grilled salmon.

A LEGACY OF FAITH + FAMILY

VINSON • JACKSON • BOONE • SEAY • ELLIS

Daddy's Hamburger and Gravy

INGREDIENTS

1 lb. fresh ground beef

1 medium onion (diced)

1 medium onion (sliced – to use in gravy)

1 green bell pepper (diced)

1 egg (beaten)

3 dashes of hot sauce

2 tsp black pepper (1 tsp for burger and 1 tsp for gravy)

1 tsp garlic powder

1 tsp onion powder

1 tsp sea salt

1 tsp browning seasoning

1 tsp chicken bouillon

1 tbsp flour

PREPARATION

In a bowl (using the best gadget in your kitchen, clean hands) gently mix the ground beef (ground turkey or chicken can be used as well), onion, bell pepper, spices and beaten egg.

Cook your burgers over medium-high heat. The burgers should sizzle when placed in the skillet. Cook to your desired wellness – in our house, well done. Set the burgers aside on a plate.

Pouring off some of the excess oil made by the burgers, leaving about 1 tbsp of the oil, add the sliced onions – allowing them to caramelize. Add flour – making sure the flour cooks through, add browning seasoning, chicken bouillon and black pepper to taste, stirring constantly. Once the gravy thickens, place the burgers back in the skillet, cover and simmer for 5 minutes, turning the burger to ensure you coat all sides with the gravy.

This was a quick weekday meal in my home or when Daddy just wanted a burger.

Serve with mashed potatoes or rice and vegetable of choice.

Easy Salmon Pasta

INGREDIENTS

2 5 oz salmon pouches

1 16 oz box of farfalle (bowtie) pasta

1 24 oz jar pasta sauce

1 cup heavy/whipping cream

½ cup shredded Parmesan and Romano cheese

1 tsp dried basil

1 tsp dried oregano

1 tsp garlic powder

1 tbsp pink Himalayan salt

1 tsp lemon pepper

1 10 oz pkg frozen green peas

½ cup roasted red peppers

2 garlic cloves (chopped)

2 tablespoon olive oil

¼ cup real bacon bits

PREPARATION

Farfalle Pasta
Follow directions on box.

Salmon
Using a medium sauce pan, sauté garlic in olive oil until warmed through; add pasta sauce, whipping cream, basil, oregano, pink salt, garlic powder, lemon pepper and green peas. Once sauces begins to bubble, add salmon, reducing heat to simmer allowing the flavors to blend.

Toss cooked pasta and salmon mixture. Sprinkle with real bacon bits.

This is a great meal maker with rotiesserie chicken, shrimp and flows well as a vegetarian dish.

Serve with crusty garlic bread and salad.

Field Peas and Snaps

INGREDIENTS

16 oz package frozen field peas and snaps
(for dried beans/peas follow the directions for soaking before cooking)

4 oz Smoked Turkey (neck, wing, drumstick — whatever you prefer)

¼ cup Chicken Bouillon*

2 Bay Leaves

1 tsp Marjoram

1 tbsp Complete Seasoning/All Purpose

1 tsp Black Pepper

4 cups water

PREPARATION

In 6 quart pot add water, smoked turkey, seasonings. Boil for 10-15 minutes or until meat is tender. Add beans or peas. Again, bring to a boil. Taste liquid to see if any additional seasonings are needed.

Reduce heat, cover pot and cook for 1 hour until beans or peas are tender creating a cloudy almost thick consistency to the broth.

This recipe is great with any type of bean or peas: Green Baby Lima Beans - Speckled Butter Beans - Crowder Peas - Purple Hull Peas - White Acre Peas, etc.

*If you're watching your sodium intake, leave out the chicken bouillon and use low sodium chicken broth in place of the water.

Great with cornbread and a glass of ice tea!

Fish Curry

INGREDIENTS

- 4 fish filets (your choice, rough cut)
- 2 tbsp olive oil
- 1 tbsp minced garlic
- ½ bell pepper (chopped)
- 1 medium onion (chopped)
- ½ tsp curry powder
- 1 tsp thyme
- 1 tsp garlic powder
- ½ tsp red pepper flakes
- 4 cups chicken broth
- ½ tsp ground flax seed

PREPARATION

Rough cut fish filets; dust with curry powder and toss to ensure each piece is lightly coated. Set aside.

In 6 quart pot caramelize onions in olive oil; adding curry powder, minced garlic; add bell peppers, allowing peppers to sweat; add chicken broth, garlic powder, thyme, ground flaxseed, red pepper flakes. Bring to a boil; add fish, reduce heat. Cook until fish is opaque in color.

Serve with brown rice.

Grace Prayer

Psalm 112, 1-2

"How blessed is the man who fears the Lord, who greatly delights in his commandments. His descendants will be mighty on earth; the generation of the upright will be blessed."

Legacy begins in your heart, through your relationship with God.

To the most high and everlasting God, my Father, we praise and lift Your holy and righteous name. We thank You for Your grace, Your undeserving mercy, and Your indisputable love. You said that if we declare a thing, it will be established for You, so light will shine on Your ways. So, Lord, we declare and decree that as Your Word lights our path, You will find favor over our families throughout the generations. We pray for salvation for the family, we pray that our families (especially the children), will fulfill their purpose in life and will think outside the box. Let us become the Psalm 1 Christian family, living out Your admonishment, "Blessed is the man who walks not in the counsel of the ungodly nor stands in the way of sinners, nor sits in the seat of the scornful, but his delight is in the law of the Lord and on his law, he shall meditate day and night. He is like a tree planted by the rivers of water that yields its fruit in its season and its leaves do not wither, and all that he does shall prosper."

Let them not forget that they are the head and not the tail; and encourage them to never settle for less than they deserve. Let their vision be clear, let them be motivated, and live in prosperous and heathy atmospheres.

Let us be living examples as our lives reflect Your glory. Let our lives be examples of the fruit of the spirit, let Your precious love define our lives. I pray that Your Holy Spirit would caress our minds and intoxicate our being as we continue to live according to Your Word. We decree and declare that You will change circumstances as we speak life in every dead situation. We are a royal priesthood, because Jesus is our Lord and King, so as we manifest our anointing, we speak powerful declarations over our family. We decree and declare these things for our family: salvation, healing, love, peace, anointing, savvy business ideas, successful negotiations, marriages, inventions, creations, products, goods and services. We declare and decree that we will not be burdened with finances, everything that we lost or is owed to us is being restored, and every generational curse is broken.

We decree and declare victory in Jesus' name over our family, and every generation that represents us. Thank You Lord for the second edition of Culinary Roots. You have allowed this to be more than a cookbook with recipes, but savory, flavorful, soulful antidotes for life. Lord God, I pray Your many blessings on Culinary Roots and on every family that encounters the recipes and family traditions chronicled. We will forever give You all the glory, and all the honor, in Your precious son Jesus' name. Amen.

Lorraine Jones
North Miami, Florida

Fried Bologna (Balonie) Sandwich

INGREDIENTS

1-2 Bologna Slices (thickness of the slice is your preference)

Non-stick cooking spray or oil

Yellow Mustard

2 Slices Toasted White Bread (or any bread – my fav is multi-grain, but we're going old school on this one)

PREPARATION

Add cooking spray or oil to a hot fry pan. If you're really doing this Old School, get out the cast iron skillet.

With a knife or kitchen scissors, make four ¼ to ½ inch cuts on the edge of the bologna. Lay in your hot skillet, cooking both side until browned to your liking.

Assembly is easy. Spread mustard on each slice of bread, placing the bologna on one slice, topping with the other slice, press, cut sandwich on the diagonal and eat.

Variations to this sandwich are infinite:

- Bologna – Mustard – Potato Chips
- Bologna – Eggs – Cheese
- Bologna – Caramelized Onions – Fresh Spinach – Sliced Tomatoes

There are those who may say, this is pedestrian and dare not serve to family or friends. My response to you is, put it on a toasted brioche bun with Dijon mustard, arugula and roasted red peppers. I think that will satisfy the "upper crust" in your circle.

Fried Cabbage

INGREDIENTS

1 large head of cabbage –
(I prefer selecting ones having the darker outer leaves as they provide good texture and color contrast)

6 slices of bacon

1 onion (chopped)

1 tsp minced garlic

2 cups chicken broth

1 tbsp Complete Seasoning

1 tsp Black Pepper

1 tbsp Balsamic Vinegar

1 tsp Cilantro

Red pepper flakes to taste

PREPARATION

Prepping Cabbage:
Removing the darker leaves from the cabbage, roll darker leaves tightly and slice into strips*. Then cut the remains of the cabbage head in half using a large knife, slice into in strips. Rinse the cabbage in cold water and drain.

In a 6 quart pot add bacon, onion and minced garlic – cook until bacon is crispy. Fry/sauté cabbage allowing the cabbage to cook down a bit. Cabbage generates water so the cooking process will release the water contained in the vegetable. Add all seasonings to taste. Stir in chicken broth, reduce heat to medium and cover. Cook for 10-20 minutes or until cabbage is tender.

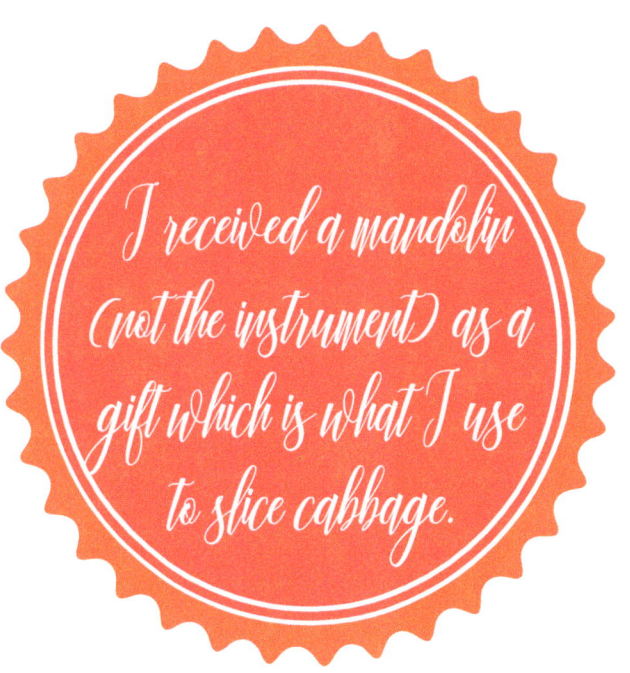

I received a mandolin (not the instrument) as a gift which is what I use to slice cabbage.

Family Celebrations

Happy Birthday Miss Vickie

She's 80 and Elegant

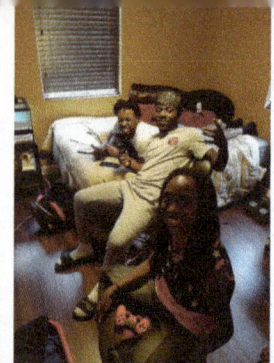

Fried Chicken Gizzards

INGREDIENTS

2 lbs chicken gizzards

2 eggs

2 tbsp water

Flour for dredging

Everglades Fish and Chicken Seasoning to taste

Panko bread crumbs

Canola, Safflower or Peanut oil for frying

PREPARATION

Rinse gizzards well.

Prepare three dipping/dredging stations: (1) flour; (2) egg mixture (2 eggs and 2 tablespoons water); and (3) panko bread crumbs.

Lightly dredge gizzards in flour; coat with egg mixture; then dredge in bread crumbs completely coating the gizzards. Continue in this order until all of the gizzards are prepped for frying.

Fry in oil until golden brown. Serve hot.

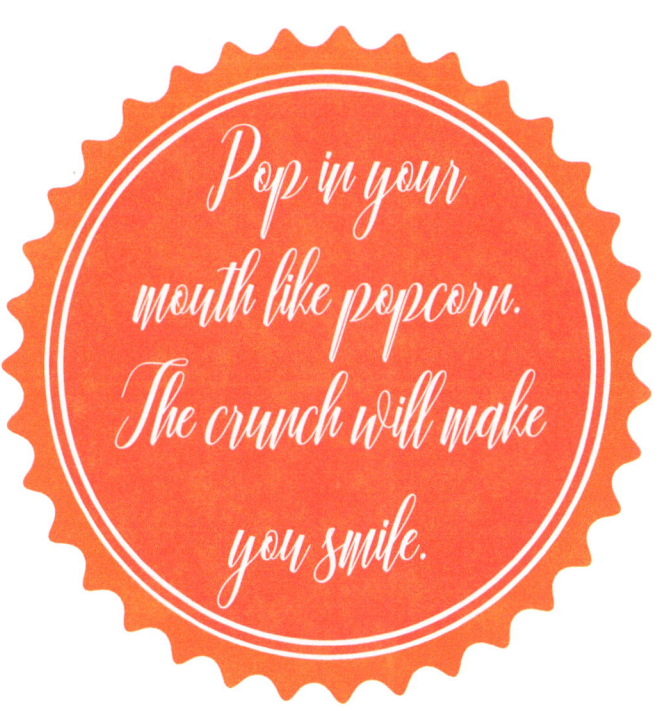

Pop in your mouth like popcorn. The crunch will make you smile.

Frittata

INGREDIENTS

10 eggs

1 12-16 oz pkg breakfast sausage

1 10 oz pkg frozen chopped spinach (thaw and remove excess water)

1 medium onion chopped

1 15 oz can sliced potatoes drained and rinsed

1 cup shredded cheddar cheese

¼ cup evaporated milk or any milk you prefer

1 tsp pink salt

1 tsp black pepper

1 tsp garlic

red pepper flakes to taste

PREPARATION

Brown sausage in a frying pan until thoroughly cooked; add chopped onion, sautéing until the onions are tender/translucent. Add in the potatoes and spinach. Set this mixture to the side to cool.

Whip eggs with ¼ cup milk add whatever seasonings you like.

Coat casserole dish with cooking spray or melted butter. Pour in meat mixture, spreading evenly in the casserole dish. Pour in the eggs; add the cheese on top.

Bake in preheated 350 degree oven for 30 minutes or until frittata is firm and cheese is golden brown.

I serve with salsa and toast points.

Green Beans and White Potatoes

INGREDIENTS

4 slices of bacon (chopped)

½ cup minced garlic

2 medium onions (chopped)

1 green bell pepper (chopped)

1 tbsp curry powder

½ tsp red pepper flakes

½ tsp black pepper

4 cans green beans (drained and rinse)

2 cups chicken broth

5 small or medium size potatoes (rough cut)

Cajun Seasoning to taste

Peanut oil for frying

PREPARATION

In a 4-quart pot bacon until crispy. Remove bacon, preserving renderings; add garlic and onions to same pan and sauté until onions are browned on the edges.

Return bacon to the pot adding bell peppers, red pepper flakes, black pepper and ½ tbsp curry powder. Continue to sauté until curry powder has browned. Add green beans, 2 cups chicken broth and simmer for 10 minutes.

Wash potatoes, pat dry with paper towel; season with Cajun seasoning and remaining ½ tbsp curry powder. Place in deep fryer or fry pan until golden brown (7-10 min).

Drain potatoes thoroughly; add to green bean mixture, tossing gently together and serve.

Mama loves green beans and potatoes.

Hodge Podge Oven Jambalaya

INGREDIENTS

2 6 oz chicken breasts (cooked and diced)

(or pick up a roasted chicken from the store – remove skin)

2 lbs andouille sausage (diagonal cut)

10 mini corn cobs

1 medium onion (sliced)

1 small bag of baby potatoes (cut in half)

16 oz bag frozen okra (optional)

Creole Seasoning to taste

½ cup Olive Oil

Red pepper flakes to taste

4 cups parboiled rice

8 cups water

Garlic powder

Onion powder

Black pepper

PREPARATION

This recipe is in homage to all the women of the Jackson and Reid family, including my Mama.

Florida Mae Victoria Reid Jackson, could always take whatever remnants of groceries were found in the refrigerator or freezer and create a meal. She passed that gift onto me.

One Sunday afternoon upon completing meal prep, I realized I had two cooked chicken breasts that I did not use. I did what my Mama would do – checked the fridge and the freezer and found the ingredients to create this recipe.

Preheat oven to 350 degrees.

In a large roasting pan (I always have disposables foil pans around – being we are a big family). Add sausage, corn, potatoes, onion, okra, creole seasoning, black pepper and red pepper flakes. Pour in the olive oil, gently tossing all the ingredients until coated throughout.

Bake uncovered for 1 hour.

Now that the oven portion is in the works – time to prepare the rice.

Bring 8 cups of water to a boil, adding chicken bouillon, garlic powder, onion powder and rice. Once pot returns to a boil, reduce heat and simmer 10-12 minutes or until the rice absorbs the liquid.

In the large roasting pan, fold in the rice and already cooked chicken into the sausage and vegetable mixture. Cover and allow it to rest for a few minutes before serving. This can also be made ahead – keeps well for 2 days. The longer it sits, the better the flavor. In my house that is the max shelf life. Although it can be gone in one, if the "crumb snatcher's" hunger level is a CODE 1 that day.

Served with a salad and iced tea only makes it better.

Mac and Cheese CR 2.0

INGREDIENTS

16 oz. Cellentani or penne pasta

2 sticks butter

1 tbsp garlic powder

1 tbsp sea salt

1 tsp black pepper

Red pepper flakes to taste

1 can evaporated milk

1 can cream of chicken soup

8 oz shredded sharp cheddar cheese

8 oz shredded mild cheese

8 oz shredded four cheese Mexican style blend

1 box cheese crackers

Make it your own adding spinach, broccoli, ham or even chicken.

PREPARATION

Follow package directions for cooking pasta. Spray baking dish with non-stick cooking spray and pour in pasta. Sprinkle and gently toss Mexican blend cheese throughout the pasta.

Cheese Sauce: iin a sauce pan melt butter; garlic powder, sea salt, black pepper, red pepper flakes. Add cream of chicken soup; stirring slowly; add evaporated milk, allowing it to slowly warm – stirring constantly. Gently add remaining bags of cheese in parts, stirring slowly. Continue to stir allowing cheese to melt and combine with the other ingredients.

Once cheese sauce is at a thick consistency and easily pourable, fold in with pasta incorporating the cheese sauce throughout.

CR 2.0:
In the first book, I used bread crumbs as my topping. This new topping gives more crunch that dazzles with the creaminess of the pasta and cheese. I hope you enjoy it!

Topping:
Using a food processor or blender, pulsing half of the box of crackers to a nice chunky consistency. A potato masher will work also. Then in the same sauce pan used for the cheese sauce melt the second stick of butter; add the crushed crackers toss and gently coating with the melted butter. Spoon on top of the blended pasta and cheese.

Bake at 350 degrees for 40-50 minutes.

Mustard and Turnips

INGREDIENTS

2 bags already cleaned and cut mustard and turnip greens*

½ lb of smoked turkey wings, necks or 1 drumstick (cut-up)

¼ cup chicken bouillon**

4-5 dashes of hot sauce

1 tbsp sugar

2 tbsp vinegar

1 tbsp garlic powder

1 tbsp sea salt

black pepper to taste

1 tbsp cilantro

½ tsp red pepper flakes

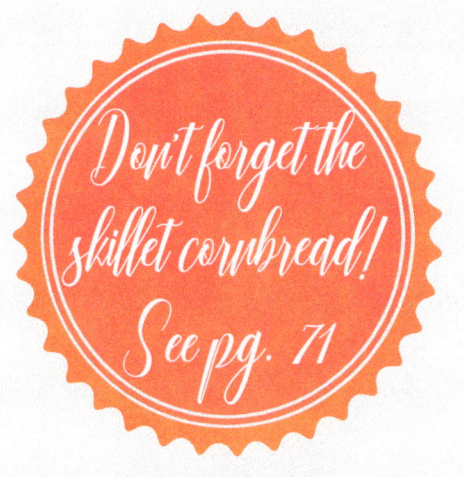

PREPARATION

Wash and rinse greens thoroughly. In large pot (4 quart) place smoked turkey, cover with water; boil for 10-15 minutes or until fork tender. Add first bag of greens and dry seasonings. As greens cook down add second bag.

Allow to slow cook for 2-3 hours or until the greens are tender.

If you like heat, add more hot sauce and red pepper flakes. If you're feeling adventurous add a scotch bonnet pepper.

*The convenience of fresh mustard, turnip or collard greens being pre-washed and pre-cut were not available in the stores as they are today. Whether we grew them in our garden or purchased from the store (bundled with the classic extra-large red rubberband to secure the stems and wrapped in newspaper for easy carry), prepping greens to cook was a tedious task. The whole leaves are pulled from the stems, placed in a sink filled with water, waiting for the dirt to settle to the bottom, rinse and repeat the process until there is no gritty feel to the leaves. Bundle 4 to 5 leaves of greens, rolling the leaves tightly, cutting in the leaves in strips.

**If you're watching your sodium intake, leave out the chicken bouillon and use low sodium chicken broth in place of the water.

Pancetta and Cheddar Biscuits

INGREDIENTS

2 cups flour

1 tbsp baking powder

½ cup shortening

1 cup Pancetta (cubed)

½ cup (4 oz) shredded cheddar cheese

1 1/3 cup milk

PREPARATION

Preheat oven to 450 degrees.

Fry pancetta until cooked thoroughly, drain oil and set aside; in a bowl, sift dry ingredients (flour and baking powder); add shortening, cut it into flour with pastry cutter or fork until you get a crumbly texture; add cheese and pancetta; gently pour in milk and mix until the dough mixture pulls away from the sides of the bowl. Allow the dough to sit for 2-3 minutes. Using a large spoon, drop dough onto a greased baking sheet about 2 inches apart.

Bake for 12-14 minutes or until golden brown.

Serve with a holiday family breakfast.

Orlando Jackson, Sr.

"Hope God may kill me." That was my daddy's catch phrase. It did not mean he wanted God to kill him. This was his way of making sure you understood how serious the words were when it came to the actions he was willing to take when it came to the well-being of his wife and children. If you hurt us, you better hope God killed him, before he got to you.

Daddy was a man of few words. His words were spoken with a tone of roughness. But, I learned (from my brilliant Mama – Florida Mae Jackson) that the hard tone was only the depth of his protection and provision for his family. He loved us the only way he knew and that was hard and heart-felt.

This drawing by his grandson, Jeremy Orlando Jackson, is the best representation of my daddy. He was a fisherman, hunter, gardener, mechanic, landscaper and so much more. The details you see in his face, arms and hands, reflect the years of hard work and determination he poured out to make sure his family had what was needed.

His legacy to us was and will always be, the love, enjoyment and protection of family, a great work ethic and to be resolute to your truth.

"Hope God may kill me."

Daddy, we love you and miss you.

Peach Cobbler

INGREDIENTS

FILLING

2 28 oz. canned peaches in heavy syrup

1 cup brown sugar

1 ½ tsp lemon extract

1 tsp vanilla extract

1 tsp cinnamon

1 tsp nutmeg

1 stick unsalted butter

CRUST

2 cups flour

1 stick unsalted butter (cold) cut in small pieces

1 cup evaporated milk (cold)

BRUSHING MIXTURE (apply to crust just before placing cobbler in oven)

½ stick butter (melted)

½ tsp cinnamon

½ tsp brown sugar

½ tsp lemon extract

PREPARATION

Combine peaches, brown sugar, lemon extract, vanilla extract, cinnamon, nutmeg and unsalted butter in a 4-6 quart pot and mix well. Bring to a boil and simmer for 20 minutes – let cool.

In a bowl, add flour and unsalted butter. Using a pastry cutter or if you're old school like me, a regular table fork will do. Cut the flour and butter together until the mixture becomes crumbly in texture. Slowly add the milk and blend until all ingredients are combined. Sprinkle flour on the cutting board; placing mixture on the board; dust with flour and then roll flat to a ¼ inch thickness. You may need to continue dusting with the flour again to ensure the crust remains manageable.

Assembly time: Preheat oven to 350 degrees - Bake time 30 to 45 minutes. Pour peaches into a 9x13 oven-safe glass or porcelain baking pan. Gently place crust on top of peaches – poke a few holes in crust which will allow the wonderful juices from the peaches to bubble to the top while baking. Finally, apply brushing mixture on top of the crust. This will provide a lovely browning effect.

CULINARY ROOTS 2

Grace Prayer

Most Righteous Father,

How can we say thanks for all that You have done? How can we express our love and appreciation for the many blessings that You so freely give us? May we never forget to say thank You, for Your bountiful blessings. We thank You for the inspiration that You have given my beloved cousin and friend, Brenda Jackson.

Lord, we thank You for the measure of faith that You have deposited into each of us, for without faith we can't please You. We thank You for the family that You have given us. A family that chooses to love, live and honor You as Lord. A family that has been so richly blessed with a legacy from our grandparents that we choose to continue. A legacy from our grandmother Georgia Reid, who in today's times would be called a "master chef"; but to us we simply knew that Grandma could make anything taste really good. We thank You for the creativity, innovation, and skills for preparing food that You have given to Brenda Jackson, a prized family possession.

I thank You that she has a desire to share her culinary creativity and skills, that she can create recipes that not only are tasty but also healthy.

I pray that this book will be a tool to the wife that desires to prepare awesome meals for her husband and family - but lacks the gift of cooking. I believe that when she serves the meals she prepares from these recipes, her family will savor the flavors. I believe that the father who desires to help his working wife will use the recipes in this book to prepare meals of love to say thank you to his wife for being a great partner. And, as she partakes of the beautiful meal prepared, may it increase unity in their marriage. I believe that single parents will find creative ways to prepare meals for their children and bring them to the table as one. I believe that caregivers will be able to watch those they lovingly take care of enjoy a meal from these recipes. I believe that caterers will be so impressed, that they will use these recipes to further their business. I believe that bloggers, food media and social media will be bombarded with great reviews and continuing referrals for Culinary Roots 2. I believe that churches who feed the homeless will use these recipes to bless those they serve. According to our faith and belief, so be it.

Now Father as this book is released, I pray that every meal that is prepared in every city, state, country from this book will be nourishing to the body, bring bonding time to families, create more around-the-table-family time and draw families closer together.

In Jesus name I pray AMEN!!!!!!

Charles A. McKnight Jr.
Orlando, Florida

Perlo Rice

INGREDIENTS

2 cups rice

4 cups low sodium chicken broth

½ lb turkey necks*

1 tbsp garlic powder

1 tbsp onion powder

1 tbsp complete seasoning

1 tbsp poultry seasoning

Black pepper to taste

PREPARATION

This recipe is about taking what's left and making another dish. When there was left over stewed chicken or neckbones, mama would make this side dish.

In this recipe, I used turkey necks that were left over. Even when there is nothing left to reinvent, you can make it without meat, using chicken broth and your preferred seasoning.

Using leftover broth from any cooked poultry add chicken broth and seasonings; bring to a boil; add rice allow to come up to boil; then simmer for 20 minutes or until liquid is absorbed by the rice.

Pork 'n Beans and Sausage

INGREDIENTS

1 LB Georgia Sausage (cut on an angle)

2-15 oz canned pork 'n beans

1 Medium Onion (chopped)

1 tsp Black Pepper

2 tbsp Brown Sugar

1 tsp Garlic Powder

½ tsp Yellow Mustard

PREPARATION

In your cast iron skillet or any frying pan you have, place sausage* and onions, cooking on medium heat until the sausage browns and the onions are translucent. Reducing the heat, add the pork 'n beans, black pepper, brown sugar, garlic powder and mustard – stir well. Let simmer until bubbling and, there is a rich color and nice consistency.

This was our Saturday meal that Mama served on top of white rice. It was economical and filling. When you have six children in the house (mostly boys), Mama cooked with the mindset of ensuring that her children were full and happy campers from their meal.

*You may notice I did not list any type of oil to cook with as sausage brings its own oil and thus creates just enough to cook the meat and the onions.

Great memories were made with this recipe.

Potato-Crusted Salmon

INGREDIENTS

2 (4-6 oz.) Salmon filet

1 cup shredded hash browns (thawed)

Lemon pepper seasoning to taste

¼ cup brown or whole grain mustard

1 cup canola oil

PREPARATION

Thaw 1 cup shredded hash browns; rinse salmon filet, pat dry with paper towel and season with lemon pepper. Coat one side of filet with mustard; press shredded hash browns on top of the mustard; allow to sit for 2-3 minutes; heat 1 cup canola oil in skillet; place salmon (potato side down) in skillet; cook on medium-high heat, 6 minutes on each side.

Serve with a nice green salad and vegetable you prefer.

Roasted Vegetable Feast

INGREDIENTS

4 medium white potatoes (rough cut)

4 medium sweet potatoes (rough cut)

1 large red onion (sliced)

1 red bell pepper (sliced)

1 green bell pepper (sliced)

1 bag petite carrots

6 mini corn cobs

¼ cup olive oil (just enough to coat vegetables)

1 tbsp thyme

1 tbsp black pepper

1 tbsp garlic powder

1 tbsp onion powder

1 tbsp pink salt

Oh yes, it's a great dish to make when you have to bring food to a gathering, especially cook-outs!

PREPARATION

After prepping and rinsing the vegetables allow them to drain for 1-2 minutes.

Place vegetables on a shallow roasting pan, adding seasonings and olive oil. Hand toss until all seasonings and olive oil have equally coated the vegetables.

Preheat oven to 400 degrees.

Roast uncovered for 1 hour. Occasionally check vegetables and shift vegetables around in pan to ensure even roasting.

These are always great with fish or chicken. On my Meatless Mondays, this dish is very satisfying.

Oh yes, it's a great dish to make when you have to bring food to a gathering, especially cook-outs!

Don't just limit yourself to the vegetables listed. I have added green beans, tomatoes, or broccoli. In homage to the line from Coming to America, "Whatever you like."

Enjoy!

Rutabagas

INGREDIENTS

2 rutabagas

4 cups of water

2 tbsps complete seasoning

2 tsps Black pepper

Red pepper flakes to taste

2 tbsps chicken bouillon

PREPARATION

Peel and rough-cut rutabagas and rinse.

Add and bring to a boil 4 cups of water into a 4-6 quart pot.

Cook on low heat for 1 ½ hours or until rutabagas are tender. Check occasionally to make sure water does not completely boil out.

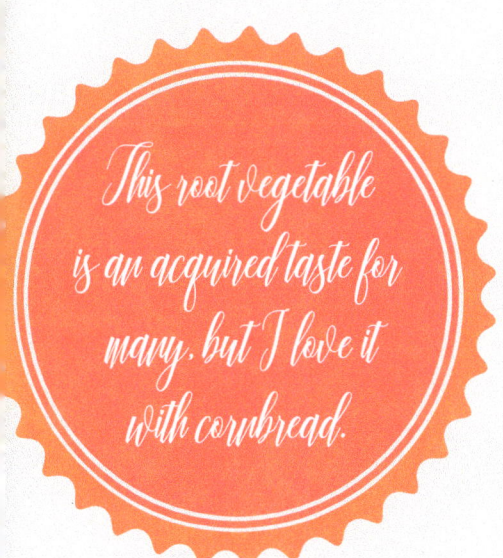

This root vegetable is an acquired taste for many, but I love it with cornbread.

Skillet Cornbread

INGREDIENTS

2 cups self-rising cornmeal

1 ½ cups buttermilk

1 tsp salt

1 large egg

Vegetable oil for frying

PREPARATION

Beat egg in bowl; add buttermilk, then salt and cornmeal – mix well.

Pour ¼ inch of oil in skillet on medium heat. Monitor the oil, so it does not smoke or pop. Pour batter into skillet (for ease of flipping pour in batches like you would pancakes), browning on both sides (3-5 minutes).

When bubbles begin to appear on upside of batter, you can safely flip and brown the other side.

Cornbread is always a great compliment to the meal, especially greens, beans and peas!

Smothered Grits

INGREDIENTS

Grits
1 cup grits

½ cup milk

2 ½ cups low sodium chicken broth

2 handfuls of fresh spinach chopped

Smother
½ lb turkey sausage or kielbasa

½ lb peeled and deveined shrimp

1 medium onion (chopped)

1 medium green bell pepper (chopped)

¼ cup extra virgin olive oil

1 tbsp flour

Low sodium chicken broth

2 tsps Complete seasoning

1 tbsp Old Bay Seasoning

Black pepper to taste

Red pepper flakes to taste

PREPARATION

Grits
Bring the chicken broth and milk to boil in a medium size pot; add grits and stir vigorously with a whisk until grits thicken; remove from heat; fold in the fresh spinach. Spoon cooked grits mixture onto a cooking spray-treated sheet pan. Place in the refrigerator for 10-20 minutes to cool – then cut into squares.

Smother
In a medium sauté pan heat olive to cook the sausage and onions. Add flour, Old Bay Seasoning, salt, black pepper and red pepper flakes. Stir until flour absorbs the oil and creates a paste (this is our roux). Pour in the chicken broth, stirring until the roux dissolves and flavors the broth. Once mixture reaches a hot temperature add shrimp and simmer for 3 minutes.

Combining
Pour and heat a thin layer of olive oil in skillet, adding 2 grit squares, browning on each side. Place the grit square on a plate; spoon smother mixture on top and enjoy!

Smother Variations:
- STEAK
- JALAPENO AND CHEESE
- CRAB
- FISH
- PORK CHOP
- CHICKEN (BONELESS SKINLESS THIGHS)

Stewed Neckbones and Potatoes

INGREDIENTS

1-2 lbs. fresh neckbones

4 medium white potatoes (rough-cut)

2 tbsp. complete seasoning

2 tbsp. chicken bouillon

2 medium onions (chopped)

1 green bell pepper (chopped)

2 tsp. browning seasoning

red pepper flakes to taste

2 bay leaves

PREPARATION

In 6-8 quart pot place neckbones and enough water to cover meat, bring to a boil.

Add other ingredients; cook on medium for 1 hour; reduce and simmer for 1 hour or until broth has rich **consistency**.

Don't forget the skillet cornbread! See pg. 71

Summer Salad

INGREDIENTS

1 head iceberg lettuce

1 cucumber (diced)

½ fresh pineapple (diced)

½ red onion (diced)

2 jalapeno peppers (seeded)

1 fresh mango (diced)

2 lime (juiced)

½ green bell peppers (diced)

½ red bell peppers (diced)

2 tbsp. sesame ginger dressing

(your preference)

A refreshing summer delight. Serves great as a side with grilled fish or chicken.

PREPARATION

Dice cucumber, pineapple, mango, onion, jalapenos, green and red bell peppers. Gently mix, squeezing the juice of 2 limes and adding dressing.

Gently pull lettuce leaves and line your platter – spooning salad mixture on top of the lettuce leaves. You can also serve the salad in a clear glass bowl. Both make a great presentation.

Quick Question:
Are you one for a hint of heat in your food? Is that a Yes? Do not seed the jalapeno. Just make sure you tell your guests in advance – enjoy!

Watermelon Cucumber Salad

INGREDIENTS

1 watermelon bowl or medium watermelon (cubed)

8 oz Feta Cheese

1 cucumber (peeled, seeded, diced)

½ cup raspberry vinaigrette

½ bag spring mix salad (rough chop)

1 lemon (juiced)

PREPARATION

In a large bowl, cut watermelon and cucumber into bite size pieces; add spring mix, feta cheese, salad dressing and lemon juice. Toss gently to coat all the ingredients.

Place in the refrigerator for 30 minutes or more before serving.

Present in your best glass bowl to show off the vibrant colors and textures of your dish.

This recipe provides a combination of sweet, salty and crunchy.

Great for summer cookouts.

Sistah Friends

Afterthought

"Just do it" is a phrase that's been popularized by the Nike brand. We have all struggled with things that have hindered us in moving on to the next phase in our journey through life. With all the distractions of outside attractions, one can only wonder how anything gets done.

These "stumbling blocks" sometimes can turn into mountains if we let them, but a strong person can overcome those hurdles with motivation and will. The catch phrase "Just do it" is one that I can identify with when describing a quality that stands out in Brenda L. Jackson (BJ to her friends).

I am honored to have the privilege of writing the afterthought on her second cookbook. If you have been blessed to read the first one, I'm sure you will be equally impressed and inspired by the contents this time. Everything shared in this book is from a caring soul. This catalog of recipes is years in the making, with BJ carefully selecting what goes into it. This also outlines, who she is and the way she is around others. A genuine warm heart, an infectious laugh and words of wisdom are only a small part of what makes her easy to love by those she interacts with.

God, family and health are what's important to her and if you know her, you are family and are loved.

Pete Billings
Hollywood, Florida

www.ingramcontent.com/pod-product-compliance
Lightning Source LLC
Chambersburg PA
CBHW061116170426
43198CB00026B/2995